Four Seasons

KHUSHI JAIN

Contents

Acknowledgement

Thank you, divine spirit, mystery of the universe for
the deep insights of lessons embedded within you.
I wish to express deep gratitude to my mother, Sabina
Jain and father, Sandeep Jain to instil within me a deeper
understanding of the world and for making me who I am.
My work would have not been done without the continual
support and vision of my editor, Sabina Jain.
My greatest appreciation is to every other professional
who made the book what it is, including Mehak Jain
and Aanchal Singal for their mesmerising artwork.
To my grandparents, Shashi Gupta, Krishna Devi
and Gianchand Jain for their blessings
To my friends, Nisha and Vanisha for always motivating
me and coming up with new ideas.
To Everyone who believed in me and shared my excitement
about this book.
Lastly, I thank all those people who took a step to show
interest and engagement to be a part of the empowering
journey. Your support means the world to me.

To the role models of my life,
Sabina and Sandeep

About the author

Khushi Jain is a multi-talented individual with a diverse range of interests and achievements. As a poet, she has enchanted readers with her evocative and heartfelt verses that explore themes of love, longing, and the human experience. A maestro of the written word, she conjures enchanting verses that dance upon the very soul, delving deep into the labyrinth of human emotions with an eloquence that is both stirring and sublime.

In addition to her literary pursuits, Khushi Jain is also an accomplished national-level shooter. With a gaze as steady

as the North Star and a hand as sure as fate, she has garnered
accolades and admiration by showcasing her exceptional skills
and dedication in marksmanship competitions.
Moreover, Khushi Jain embarks on the noble quest for knowledge
and justice as she pursues a degree in law, navigating the intricate
corridors of legal scholarship with a discerning intellect and
an unwavering commitment to fairness and equity.
Through her poetry, marksman skills, and legal aspirations,
she continues to inspire and captivate those around her, leaving
an indelible mark on the world.

Author's note

Seasons mirror the ebb and flow of life itself, each phase bringing a unique essence to our existence enhancing our growth and self realisation. It seeds the tree of hope bringing along the lessons of endurance and self growth.

From having a strong influence on ensuring food supply to the cultural practices, rhythm of seasons showcase it all. Nature within its depth also highlights the cycle of human emotions. Not all days are good, not always one can be happy is what nature preaches by the cycle of seasons.

Every bond, everything is aligned with the universe and would take its own time to arrive. Right meaning is attached with each season.

Autumn marks an age of separation and loss of bonds offering time to introspect. **Winter** then brings endurance, for it offers time to become strong through surviving in harsh weather. **Summer**, with its abundant warmth, fosters growth and allows crops to mature. It teaches the lesson of accepting the truth and preparing yourself to start afresh after going through all the pain which is to make you strong that life brings. **Spring** finally marks a period of transition, a time of renewal that awakens plant life, leading to blossoming flowers and a resurgence. It comes with happy days, new bonds and most importantly a new and resilient you.

Similarly, you can't get the right thing which is meant for tomorrow, today. Consequently, every phase has its own time and reason.

Each season turns, each phase in line,
A purpose clear, a grand design

Autumn

Autumn

In autumn's grasp of gold and red,
The leaves dance lightly, overhead
Learn the lesson it teaches,
Rule of falling apart, it preaches
With the hushed cry it notes,
Loneliness and sleepless night it denotes
While the bonds remain at play,
Uncertainty it keeps at way
In every leaf that gently falls,
There lies a story of a secret call

Tangled Hearts

I still remember;
Those endless calls,
Wrapped with laughter
Those sleepless nights,
Converged our souls,
Weaving a lifetime bond

I still hear your voice so clear,
Ready to hold my hand
Entwined in love and trust,
May our spirits forever weave

But the time waits for none,
Bonds weaken and change one
To strike a balance, we must learn to let go,
To cherish the moment but also to grow

Nourish the memories fossilised,
Leave the imprints unrealised
Embrace the memories with a big smile,
But let your heart accept the truth
Memories are to be cherished,
Just like remorse is to be perished

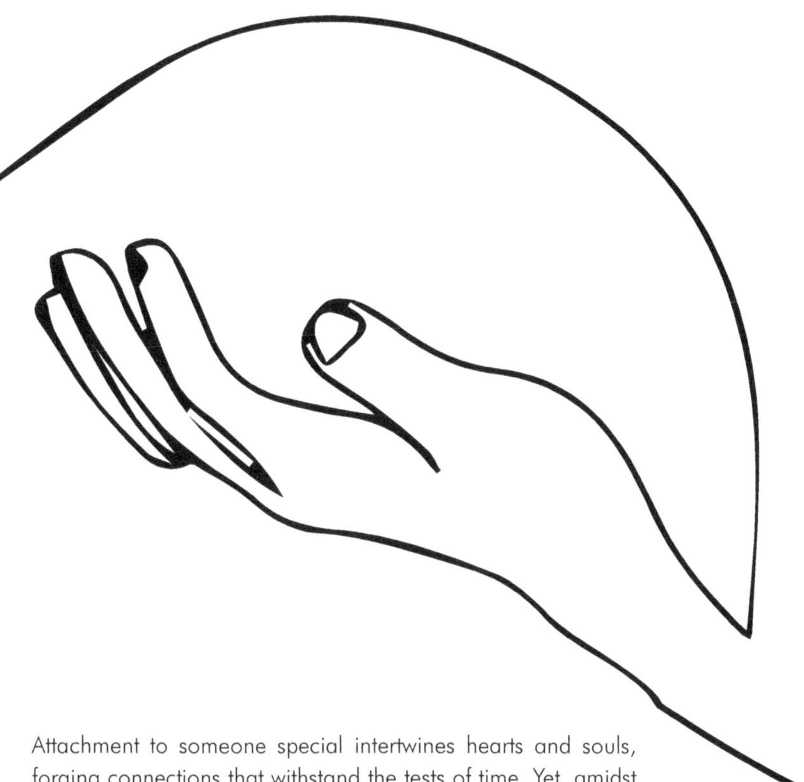

Attachment to someone special intertwines hearts and souls, forging connections that withstand the tests of time. Yet, amidst the beauty of togetherness, there are moments when the inevitable happens, and paths diverge, leading to separation and sorrow. It weighs heavily upon the heart, leaving behind echoes of laughter and whispers of shared dreams. While the pain of separation may seem insurmountable, it serves as a catalyst for growth and renewal. The void left by the absence of our someone special becomes a canvas upon which we paint the colours of our own identity, rediscovering passions and dreams long forgotten.Though the journey of parting may be fraught with sadness, it is also a moment of beauty—a testament to the depth of our attachment and the resilience of the human spirit.

Unveiling The Beauty Of Loneliness

I still miss those old days,

Filled with love and care

But separated with longings in the heart,

Those perished bonds never rejuvenated,

Those friends never came back same

Forcing me,

To embrace solitude's gentle hand

The hand became a guiding light,

Harnessing my inner core,

From the cacophony of the worldly pour

Separation is an inescapable part of life's journey. It may bring sorrow and longings, yet it teaches us the value of presence and the ephemeral nature of time. In moments of separation, we find solace in memories and hope to come out stronger. Missing your special bonds and holding memories alive does no bad unless you refuse to accept it as a part and parcel of your life.

The September

It took away the old,

Which I wished to somehow hold

With sombre and regret it came,

The cycle of life it blame

SEPTEMBER

S	M	T	W	T	F	S

Midnight Murmurs:
Moonlit Confessions

As my eyes met the moon,

I could hear the stars whispering tune

Calling me if I was fine,

But sad was I to break the laid line

For it escorted the unleashed hush,

Which were hidden beside a dense bush

There was a story of mine,

Measured by some twinkling sign

It descended my numbed eyes,

Pouring the comfort in every corner of rise

But with it accompanies pain,

With no space to drain

In the hushed embrace of night, when the world sleeps and the stars whisper secrets to the sky, there is a solace in the luminous glow of the moon. With a heart heavy and a soul burdened by sorrow, the silent sentinel of the night listens to every bit of you. Under the gentle gaze of the moon, pouring out the deepest sorrows, the unspoken burdens, feels like releasing them into the ethereal arms of the night. With each whispered confession, there is a fleeting sense of relief, a cathartic release that eases the weight upon shoulders.

The moon listens, its silent presence a beacon of comfort in the lonely hours of the night. It offers no judgement, no solutions—only a silent witness to the pain that resides within the depths of the soul. In this exchange, there's a sacred bond forged between the grieving heart and the celestial guardian above—a bond that transcends words and transcends time.

Conundrum Of Uncertainty

Uncertain are the things,

That the life brings

Uncertain are the incidents,

That are somehow reticent

For a storm destroying lands,

Learn to hurdle it with open hands

For it is uncertainty, that teaches,

Dissipate the fears, it preaches

Uncertainty is a constant companion, lurking behind every decision we make and every path we choose to follow. It whispers in our ears, reminding us that tomorrow is never guaranteed and that change is the only constant. Embracing uncertainty can be daunting, but it also holds the promise of unexpected opportunities and new beginnings.

Silent Whispers

All of us have an end,

Not always a happy blend

Tired I am to pretend,

The efforts that I send

With which comes the heavy descend,

That it forever lend

For it buried a deep chapter intend,

With no plausible end

But after every fend,

Comes a lesson to comprehend

Never conclude it as waste spend,

As every end leads to a transcend

Choosing to step away or bring something to an end doesn't diminish the effort we've already put forth or invalidate the progress we've made. It's simply a recognition that our energy and resources are finite, and we must allocate them wisely to maintain balance and harmony in our lives.

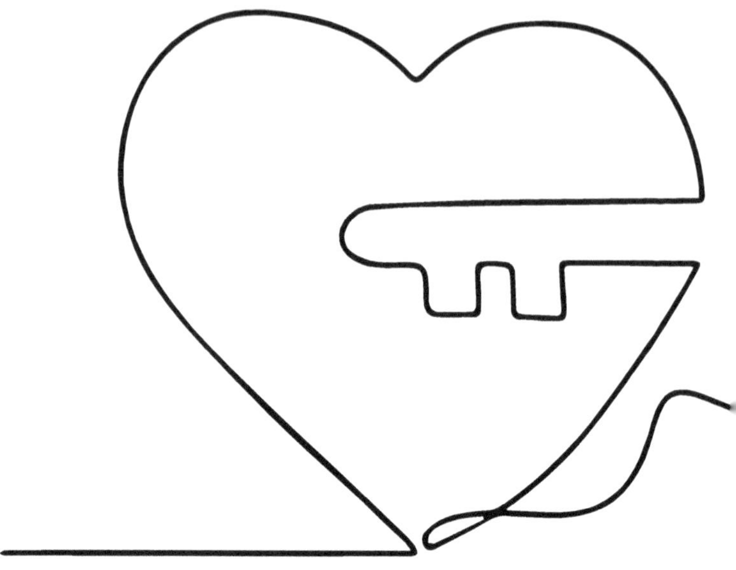

Whisper Of Gossamer Bonds

Precious are the bonds filled with love,

Grown with care and some warmth

Allure you to lock it in your pages,

And here comes the story of the ages

Transitory are the bonds,

But permanent are the haunts

Heal those embedded wounds,

Depart those painful bounds

Urge your inner soul lighting your path,

To bear all the aftermath and some wrath

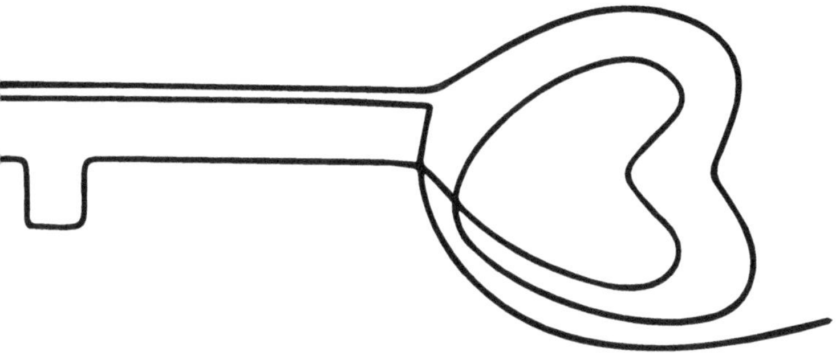

Special bonds hold a unique place in our hearts, often representing deep connections. But, there are moments when the separation of these bonds becomes necessary for our own growth and well-being. It can be a painful and difficult process to say goodbye to someone who has been a significant part of our journey, but sometimes letting go is the only path towards healing and self-discovery. By recognizing that some relationships may no longer serve us or align with our values and aspirations, we must empower ourselves to move forward with courage and resilience.

Not Now

I am not ready;
For the hard bleak,
Which my soul is urging to speak
For the naked truths,
Which play- up the accompanied ruth

I am not ready;
To face the vivid care,
Which we all somehow share
To embrace the real,
Which unfolds a mere appeal

I am not ready;
To forget my past,
Which every second suffocates and blast
To welcome a new day,
Which is full of turns at bay

May time become a gentle healer
Aiding in forms of relinquishment
Resurrecting my broken life with accomplishment

Sometimes, life can feel like a race that moves at a pace faster than we're prepared for. In these moments, it's okay to acknowledge that we're not quite ready to join the hustle and bustle of the world around us. We might need some time to gather our thoughts, strengthen our resolve, and find our footing before we can confidently step onto the track. Though it may feel daunting to pause while others surge ahead, it's important to trust that our journey is unfolding exactly as it should. In giving ourselves the gift of time, we afford ourselves the opportunity to explore our passions, set intentions, and align our actions with our deepest values.

The October

With each approaching farewell,

I rang sullen bell

Broken was I,

To even sigh

OCTOBER

S	M	T	W	T	F	S

Doubtful Ifs

Thick are the woods,

Of ifs, hiding all the goods

The suffocating doubtful sorrow,

Questions my worth morrow

In this life's dense lease,

I am trying to find my peace

Within the mysterious yard,

Lies the life whispered by bard

Doubts can cloud our perceptions, making it challenging to see the positives that exist alongside them. However, it is during these moments of doubt and confusion that the quest for inner peace becomes all the more crucial. Finding peace amidst doubts requires patience, self-reflection, and a willingness to confront and address the sources of uncertainty. It involves delving deep into our thoughts and emotions, untangling the web of doubts that hold us back, and seeking clarity and reassurance from within.

Wakeful Moonlight

Sufferings of my heart,

Leave me alone with sleepless blart

All my dreams denied,

Threaten me with scary nightmares beside

Time has come to gather tons of dare,

Embracing to discover the mystical flare

Let the soul of world test,

Proffering your best

As the darkest hour of night ways to dawn,

Awarding deep slumber's soothing lullaby yawn

In the shroud of a scary night, when shadows dance and fears take flight, it's easy to lose sight of the promise that lies just beyond the horizon. Yet, even in the darkest hours, there is a glimmer of hope, a faint whisper of dawn breaking through the veil of darkness. For every night must eventually give way to dawn, every storm must pass, and every fear must yield to the light. And when the first ray of sun pierce the sky, illuminating the world with their gentle warmth, remember that it is the culmination of the journey through the night, a testament to your strength and perseverance.

Asundered Ties

Separation was never demanded,

Yet it came granted

Maybe a rule of life,

For every bond has a lowlife

The surrounding solitude along,

Stays with prolong

Diminish the sombre notion,

Replacing with elated emotion

Through the trials of separation, we shall grow,

Stronger and wiser, with hearts that know

Separation, a rule of life that often brings tears and heartache. It is a reminder that nothing lasts forever and that change is an inevitable part of our journey. In the tapestry of existence, people come into our lives for a reason, a season, or a lifetime. Some departures are temporary, serving as catalysts for growth and change, while others are more permanent, leaving indelible imprints on our hearts and souls. Regardless of the circumstances, each separation holds valuable lessons to be learned.

The Empty Me

The scary night talks,

About the hustle, it walks

It contemplates deep,

For an instant peep

These cries hold questions today,

Seeking answers filled with comfort everyday

With a heavy heart and echoes again,

I assure my presence vain

In the shallowness of night, when shadows dance with eerie whispers and the world is cloaked in darkness, there are moments when fear grips the heart with an icy hand. It's in these harrowing hours that the mind becomes a battleground, where unanswered questions echo like haunting cries in the silence but your very presence is enough to assure the resilience you endure.

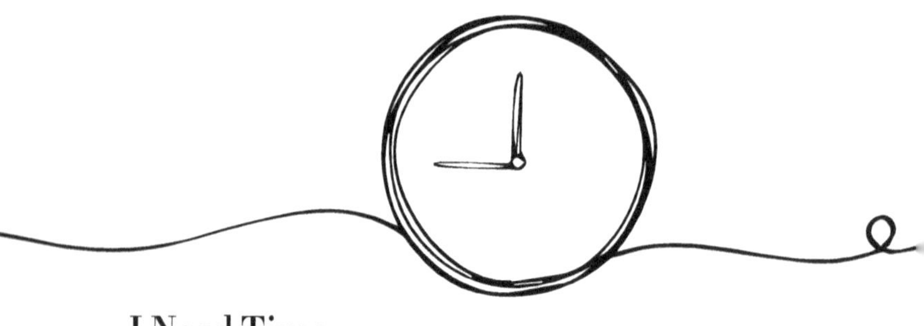

I Need Time

I need time;

To stop the harnessing blair,

For it deep down withholds the empathy of care

To absorb the sympathy that someone lend,

For it acts as the double edged sword that bend

 I need time;

To scatter the faulty attention,

For it breathes the denial mansion

To embrace the held dew,

For it submerges a weak crew

I need time;

To heal the scars,

For it holds memory hours

To come out of my cage,

For it wings the new page

Believe in time's love,

Seeding hope, and gentle sweet dove

As humans, we always wish to come out of despairing circumstances quickly. Consequently, we end up grabbing ourselves in a loop filled with delusions. Those unhealed injuries take time to cure. It is perfectly fine to give yourself moments to come back stronger. Time helps to fill the void further making you whole again. It has the remarkable ability to mend the wounds, soothe aching hearts, and rejuvenate weary souls. Just believe in the magical powers of time.

Winter

Winter

Within the depths of winter rare,

There lies a strong care

It whispers hards,

Inviting the bards

With the chilling frost it notes,

Endurance and growing strong it denotes

Healing begins, in its raucous press,

From shattered dreams to renewed caress

Sudden Scars

The sobbing sudden pain,
Came with a deep stain
Refusing further to leave,
While amending a knot's weave

Stop counting the moments so,
It take to heal the low
For there lies a purpose hidden,
In every embark glidden

The journey may feel like,
Impossible to explain alike
But the destination may feel like,
Possible to cherish alike

For even the air holds,
The power to drown bolds
Nonetheless the water lose,
The strength to excuse

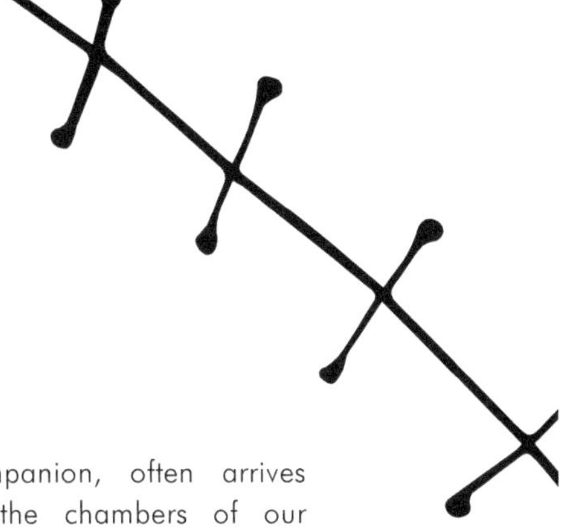

Pain, an unwelcome companion, often arrives unannounced, settling in the chambers of our hearts like an uninvited guest. It wraps around us, refusing to release its grip, casting shadows that seem endless. In the depths of despair, it's hard to imagine a life beyond its suffocating presence.Yet, in the midst of darkness, there lies a glimmer of hope, faint but resilient. With time, the sharp edges of pain begin to soften. As the days pass, we find ourselves emerging from the shadows, basking in the warmth of newfound light. And though pain may linger, it can never overpower the indomitable spirit that resides within us, guiding us towards a future filled with hope and possibility.

The January

It preached me lessons,
To start anew
Whispered to leave dark,
To embrace the triumphant mark
It held my hand, imparting right,
And whispered a symphony of light

JANUARY

S	M	T	W	T	F	S

Fears: The Hinderance Within

Face it, chase it, win it,

Nothing to be felt insecure about

Hear the knock on your ear,

Vanish the grip of your fear

Whisper the gentle words of boldness,

Transcending to quell your darkness

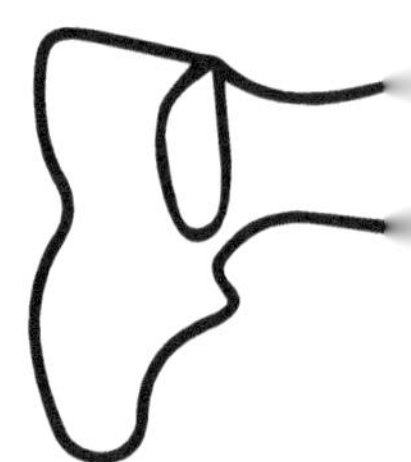

Frosting Summers

There are days who don't know,

The longings would forever snow

As are the hearts who sometimes learn,

To hate with a rage burn

But then comes the day,

With the clear and pure pray

As are the hearts that recall,

To cherish peace and happiness of all

There are days when sadness casts its shadow over our hearts, enveloping us in its sombre embrace. Yet, even in the darkest of nights, there is a glimmer of hope, a promise of brighter days to come. For just as the pendulum swings from sorrow to joy, so too does happiness emerge from the depths of despair, like a beacon guiding us home.

The Hardships

Challenges you need to be ready of

May it become a stick

Supporting you strengthen your unlimited potentials

Helping you cherish and adore every moment

Make none less than sky your limit

Let the world be amazed looking at you

For it is the hard that make you hard

Challenges, like storms on a turbulent sea, test the very fabric of our being, threatening to overwhelm us with their sheer force. Yet, within the heart of adversity lies an opportunity for growth and transformation. Each obstacle we encounter becomes a stepping stone, propelling us forward on our journey of self-discovery. Every setback becomes a lesson, every failure a stepping stone towards success.

Vicious Expectations: Hushed Killers

Realm of expectations from other,

Give rise to bother

Free yourself; self sufficiency being the key,

In the vast sea of glee

Set your soul free,

Realise your true value tree

Expectations, though often perceived as harmless guides or motivators, can quietly morph into insidious adversaries, stealthily eroding our peace of mind and sabotaging our relationships. Like hushed assassins, they lurk in the shadows of our subconscious, silently setting traps that undermine our happiness and well-being. However, expectations may be hushed killers, but we possess the power to silence their whispers and reclaim our sovereignty over our lives.

Trembling Shadows: Clutches Of Apprehension

Where my anxiousness dwells,

Nervousness as a mixed notion swells

Holding some guilt and some fear,

Spelling hard in my ear to bear

Acting as a pulsating reminder ire,

Alarming every faction a desire

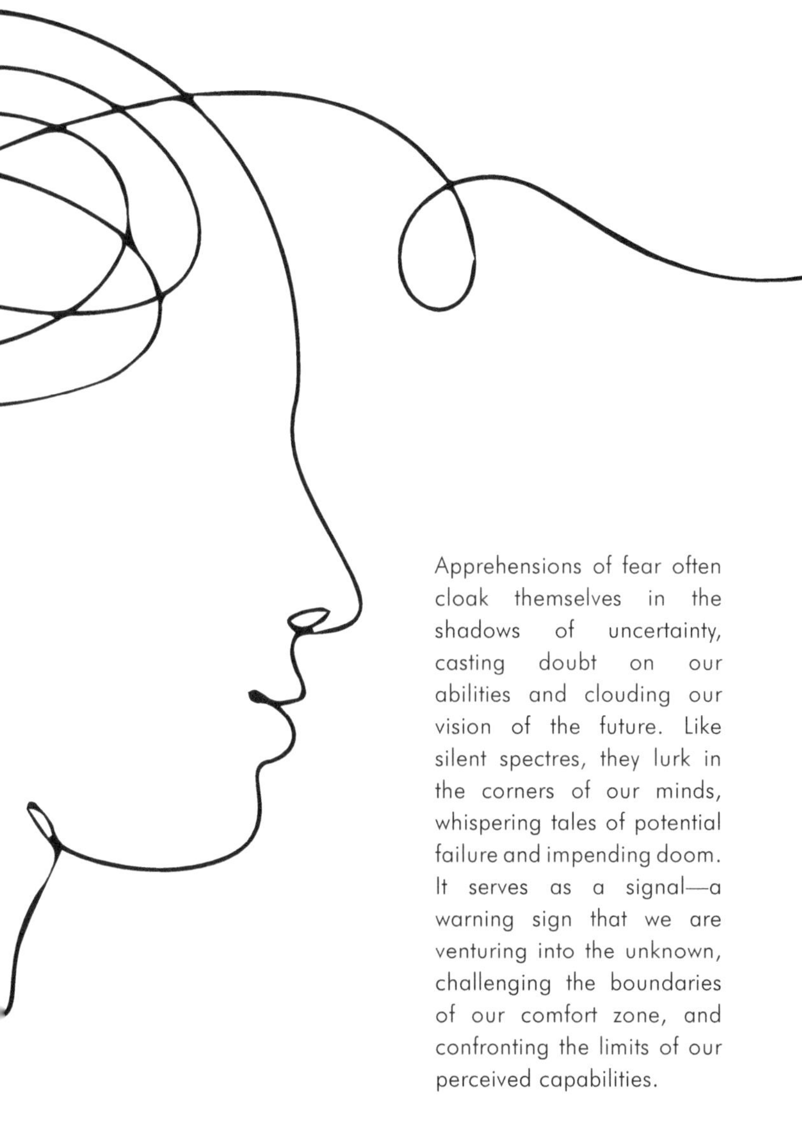

Apprehensions of fear often cloak themselves in the shadows of uncertainty, casting doubt on our abilities and clouding our vision of the future. Like silent spectres, they lurk in the corners of our minds, whispering tales of potential failure and impending doom. It serves as a signal—a warning sign that we are venturing into the unknown, challenging the boundaries of our comfort zone, and confronting the limits of our perceived capabilities.

Constant Change

Transitory is the human life,

And the bonds that perish

Transitory are the ups and downs,

And the feeling of despair

Accept it's inevitability,

Nothing to be felt insecure about

In the grand symphony of life, change is the only constant melody, weaving its way through the fabric of existence with relentless persistence. Just as the seasons transition from spring to summer, from autumn to winter, so too do our lives undergo constant transformation, each moment a fleeting snapshot in the ever-unfolding tapestry of time.

The February

It taught me to trust,
Time's healing gust
For scars need to be healed,
To grow afresh yield

FEBRUARY

S	M	T	W	T	F	S

Perish Or Cherish

Time flies here and there,

And, leaves the after-death riddles bare

Is it a soul or an end,

Hits my body's blend

Was it something before or after,

Shatters my sane rafter

Will it perish or cherish,

Traps the innocent me in a squarish

Let's not try to bare the hidden,

For it is purposely forbidden

Something great lies beneath,

As it is the energy's heat

Doubts about the afterlife are a natural part of the human experience, stemming from the inherent uncertainty that surrounds what lies beyond the realm of the known. While it's only natural to ponder the mysteries of existence, dwelling too much on the uncertainty of what comes next can sometimes overshadow the beauty and richness of the present moment.

Crimson Amber: Rustle Reverie

When lies no one to lend you a shoulder,
Ways to the emotions colder
May moon be your listener,
With you the storyteller
Breathe the true- you here,
With all the care
For it never goes in vain,
Neither lends any pain
Like the leaves of tree,
Grow more radiant as a bairn wee

In the serene embrace of the night, amidst the soft glow of the moon, there exists a sacred space for solace—a sanctuary where one can unburden the weight of their sorrows and emerge stronger, fortified by the gentle light of understanding. Each whispered confession becomes a step towards healing, a release of pent-up emotions that allows the soul to breathe freely once more. Like the phases of the moon, life is marked by cycles of darkness and light, of loss and renewal. It is a reminder that even in our darkest moments, we are never truly alone, for the moon stands as a silent witness to our pain, our struggles, and our triumphs.

Self Vs. Them

Is it my coffee's touch,
Or the rain's slutch
That completes me

Is it my spell,
Or someone else's shell
That elates me

Is it my kindness gentle,
Or others' generous sentimental
That lends the fruits to me

Is it my fulfillers great,
Or there's emptiness crate
That carves the whole out of me

Dilemma of self and them,
Leaves with a doubtful stem
But in the battle of self versus them,
I'll always choose to be the gem.

In the labyrinth of life, amidst the twists and turns of fate, there often arises a perplexing question: Is it our own efforts, our work, our choices that shape the course of our lives, or do external forces and contributions play a more significant role in determining our destiny? At times, it's easy to believe that our successes and failures are solely the result of our own endeavours. Yet, in moments of reflection, we realise that we are but threads in the intricate tapestry of existence, woven together by the interplay of countless factors and forces.

In the end, it is about finding solace in the understanding that while we may not have all the answers, we are each the architects of our own destiny, guided by the interplay of our efforts and the contributions of the world around us.

Essence Within

Soul controls everything

Unveils the facade nithing

Try not to fool

Control it to keep your cool

With patience, analysis, and gentle grace,

Solve the riddle present in this space.

The soul stands as a bastion of immense strength—an intangible yet formidable force that shapes our perceptions, drives our actions, and navigates the complexities of life with unwavering resolve.

The December

It held my hand,

To help me cherish

Although it marks an end,

Yet epitomes a major amend

DECEMBER

S	M	T	W	T	F	S

Pulse Of My Being

Some hearts never learn to hate,

For they always spread love straight

The place they hold,

Is full of purity and bold

The place my heart holds in my body,

Is not the same in my life

The way it guides my blood,

Is not the same as it guides my emotions

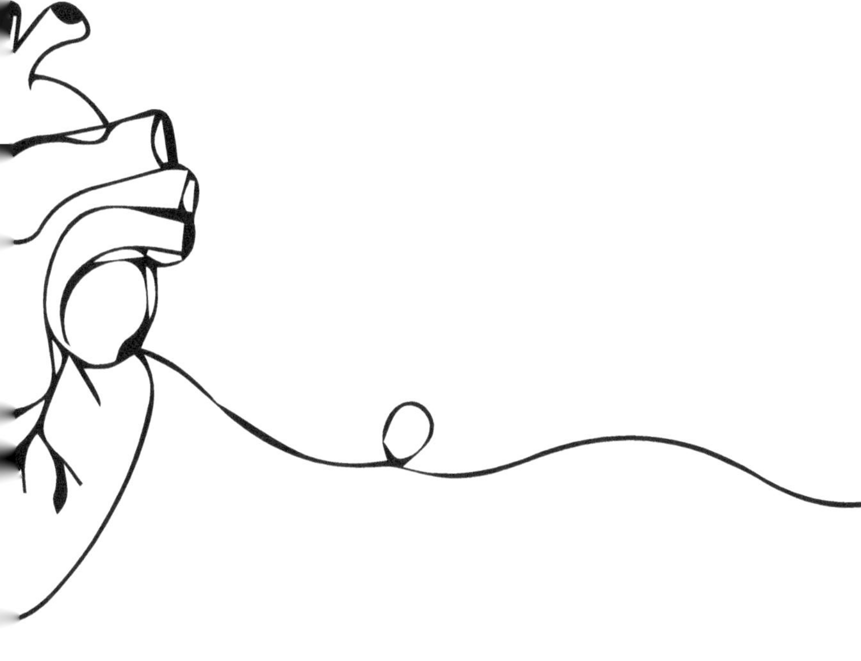

Oh! My dear heart, you beat to the rhythm of love, pulses echoing with the intensity of emotion and passion. Yet, unlike the orderly flow of blood through the veins, you don't always guide emotions in straight, predictable paths. Why do you trouble me? You force me to deal with the full spectrum of emotions, from the soaring heights of joy to the depths of despair, with a courage and vulnerability that is both exhilarating and terrifying. Why do you do so? Oh! My dear heart.

SUMMER

Summer

In the heart of summer's golden haze,

Where sunlit skies in azure rays

The oceans sparkle, waves arise,

Reflecting clear, cerulean skies

It embraces the truth though,

And empowers to accept so

For strength lie in eyes wild

Not in the delicate mild

With every dawn, the warmth renews,

A season dressed in vibrant views

Surge And Swell

Waves always enticed me,

Born with the power acquired thee

As they rise and soar,

Leaves imprints with much larger roar

But when the night prevails,

They turn into secrets and tales sail

In their ceaseless motion, we find release,

A reminder to surrender and find peace

Waves, with their rhythmic ebb and flow, symbolise a duality that mirrors the complexities of life itself. At once, they embody both strength and calmness, being a testament of the resilience of nature and the serenity found within its embrace.

The June

It reflects a stage,

When you are struck in middle age

But it gives a new rise,

If managed with delicate wise

JUNE

S	M	T	W	T	F	S

Success

Success an epitome of a game of cards,

A game of chance,

Enshrining millions of possibilities & opportunities

Flip your cards & you will see all being in your favour,

Fall into the infiniteness of the mysterious universe

Success is a journey marked by perseverance, passion, and purpose—a destination sought by many, achieved by few, and defined by each individual's unique aspirations and values. It is not a linear path but a series of trials, tribulations, and triumphs, a journey marked by setbacks, failures, and moments of doubt.

Beyond Us

God; a power behind all the fascinations

Not a definite figure but something evocative

Lies amongst us

With incredible powers

Feel the power, admire it

Let it bolster you in all your hards

Believing in God is like feeling the warmth of the sun on your face, even when clouds obscure its light. It's an unshakable conviction that there is a higher power, a divine presence that guides, sustains, and embraces us in the tapestry of existence. This belief is a beacon of hope in the darkest of nights, a source of strength when faced with life's uncertainties.

Okayness

It is okay;

To be at your low,

As it might await a destiny so

To cry shedding tears,

As it's the soul's release for years

It is okay;

To sleep with heavy past,

As the new day dawns vast

To cling the hain pain,

As the flower holds both sun and rain

It is okay;

To be quiet near,

As the unsaid says clear

To be affected from shouldn't,

As shattered you wouldn't

It takes courage to acknowledge when the weight of the world feels heavy upon our hearts and the burdens of life seem overwhelming. In these moments, it's okay to retreat into the solace of sleep, allowing ourselves the respite needed to process our emotions and find the strength to carry on.

The Tenacious We: Outsetting Endurance

In realm of hards,

Lies the tale of bards

Strong are we,

Prepared to face vast sea

Diligent are we,

To embrace the waiting glee

Neither exists here a room of doubt,

Nor any accompanied bout

For we are a warrior; armed and brave,

Facing adverse; we shine and we pave

AND here comes an another day of

YOU being

more Powerful, more Experienced & more Resilient

Embracing inner strength is like discovering a hidden reservoir of power within yourself—a wellspring of courage and determination that empowers you to face life's challenges with grace and fortitude. It's about trusting your inner voice and listening to the wisdom of your heart. With each passing day, you grow stronger, more resilient, and more empowered to face whatever challenges come your way.

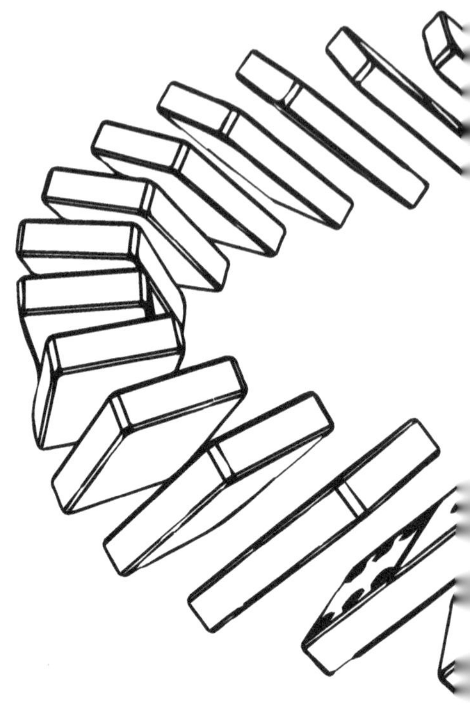

Karma: A Backscattering Cycle

Karma holds deeds in its cage,

Waiting to turn the page

Measures the intent of our eyes,

Ready to catch lies

Bonafide never goes in vain,

Neither lends any pain

In the world full of stories to tell,

Karma decides the way to heaven or hell

Karma, the ancient concept that transcends cultures and beliefs, is often described as the cosmic law of cause and effect. It suggests that our actions, thoughts, and intentions have consequences that reverberate through the universe, shaping our present and future experiences. At its core, karma teaches us accountability and responsibility for our choices. It reminds us that every action we take, no matter how small or seemingly insignificant, carries weight and leaves an imprint on our journey through life. It invites us to live with awareness, humility, and a sense of reverence for the intricate web of life in which we are all woven.

Shifting The Focus

Reason for my trigger unfolds,

Where the fear of self worth unfurls

Restless are my eyes,

Seeking the true suffice

Shift the blame game,

From dying to igniting flame

Embrace the life as it is,

From desolating to celebrating bliss

Not doubting your self-worth signifies an act of self-love and empowerment—a recognition of your inherent value, your unique gifts, and the beauty that resides within you. It's about cultivating a deep sense of respect and appreciation for yourself, regardless of external validation or approval and embracing your authenticity, owning your truth, and standing tall in the knowledge that you are enough, just as you are. You just need to shift your focus from doubting the circumstances life entails to actually living them.

Serenading Self Acceptance: The Mirror Within

IT IS OKAY TO not to be okay,

IT IS OKAY TO feel lonely ,

Leave behind the haunting haze of pain,

Running behind perfectionism go in vain

The little imperfectness within accomplishes you,

For bliss lies in being perfectly imperfect

In a world that often celebrates perfection, it's important to remember that it is okay to be imperfect. Imperfection is not a flaw to be hidden or ashamed of; rather it is a reminder that we are all unique individuals, each with our own strengths, weaknesses, and quirks that make us.

The July

In its arms, we learn to see,
The beauty in all that comes to be
Through trials fierce and storms that roar,
Acceptance stands, steadfast, at the core

JULY

S	M	T	W	T	F	S

I Can And I Will

A doubtful night full of ifs,

Ways to desperate sniffs

Spark the flame of horrible night,

Ignite the soul's extinguished light

Belief and trust being the way,

Sets the problems at bay

In the face of daunting obstacles and unforeseen hurdles, trusting in oneself becomes an anchor—a steadfast conviction that no matter the odds, you possess the power and tenacity to overcome. It is a mindset that fosters resilience, resourcefulness, and a willingness to embrace the unknown with courage and optimism.It is a reminder that you are capable, resourceful, and deserving of success in all your endeavours.

Echoes Of Existence

In the depths of hardship,
Beacon of realisation saved by ship
Every down will have an up's wood,
Just like every bad day would lead to good
Revealing a power untold,
Will force a story to unfold

The Unsaid Said

Silence is to be heard,
Amidst the chaos and whirred
Revere the silent hours
Cherish the blooming flowers
It speaks of peace, it speaks of calm,
A quietude that heals all harm

Silence, in its profound depths, often carries the weight of unspoken words, a language unto itself that speaks volumes without uttering a sound. It's in the hushed moments between conversations where emotions linger, where thoughts echo in the chambers of the heart, seeking expression in the quietude. So, let us embrace the silence, for within its hallowed space, words find their meaning, and understanding blossoms like a flower in the quiet garden of the soul.

Eternal Sunshine

Joy lies in small,
And is different for all,
While also bounces life's ball

In the dawn's warmth you receive,
Wholeheartedly you perceive,
For joy is about the way you conceive

From child's eyes,
To birds overwhelming flies,
Joy has its roots allies

It is not a destination weak,
But a journey to seek,
For it transpires every 7 days a week

Happiness is not a fleeting emotion or a destination to be reached but a state of being —a treasure that we carry with us wherever we go, lighting up the darkest corners of our lives and guiding us on a journey of meaning, purpose, and fulfilment.

The August

In its' strong wake,

Lies every step one takes

The days that kissed,

Are always missed

AUGUST

S	M	T	W	T	F	S

Daring To Be Fearless

Drown in the air,

Like a warrior in the blair

For it paves the way,

With the regret away

A look at the eyes,

Empowers to accept all the flawed lies

Spring

Spring

In fields of green, where flowers bloom,

Comes forth a season, dispelling gloom

It whispered a new start,

To revel life's chart

With gentle dilemma and wait,

Spring emerges as a purest date

In every bud and every tree,

Lies the adorable and admirable sea

For it offers the way to flourish,

The bonds' symphony, it nourish

You: The Central Character

It was never due to you
As the words they use,
Showcase their amuse
You were not at fault; ever,
But no-fault liability exists hether

It was never due to you
As the actions they commit,
Whisper their temper emit
They have a beautiful soul,
But traumas and teachings scroll

It was never due to you
As the experiences add in rack,
And, simultaneously it reflects back
They do have good memories,
But the bad metamorphosis into ivories

It was never due to you

As their behaviour endowed,

Forms a cognition eroded

They might have mens rea (1) short,

But actus rea (2) holds no excuse forth

It was never about them

As the emotions you hold,

Shape your core's mould

The peace that is instilled,

Surely pays you back distilled

Nurturing existing bonds and safeguarding inner peace requires an understanding that extends beyond the confines of our own perspective. It entails recognizing that the actions and choices of others are not always a reflection of our worth or significance. Instead, they are manifestations of their own journey, shaped by experiences, beliefs, and emotions unique to them. Maintaining inner peace amidst the ebb and flow of relationships requires a willingness to release the need for control and surrender to the inherent unpredictability of human interactions. We learn to celebrate the uniqueness of each individual's journey, finding solace in the knowledge that true harmony arises from a place of genuine acceptance and understanding. Also, the incidents of your life and the way you behave are repercussions of your emotions, and are not always about them.

It was thus not always due to you.

The March

It felt like a rain's touch,
Which was a gentle reminder
It washed away the old,
And ignited the bold

MARCH

S	M	T	W	T	F	S

Unfolding The True Me

'I' a single letter word,

But a sturdy sword

Guide your steps when the shadow bid adieu,

Love it, care for it , prioritise it

As the most amazing creation of God,

Celebrate the true essence of you being true you

Unfolding the true essence of oneself involves peeling back the layers of conditioning, expectations, and societal norms to reveal the radiant core of our being—the essence of who we truly are.

Delving Into The Beauty Of Nature

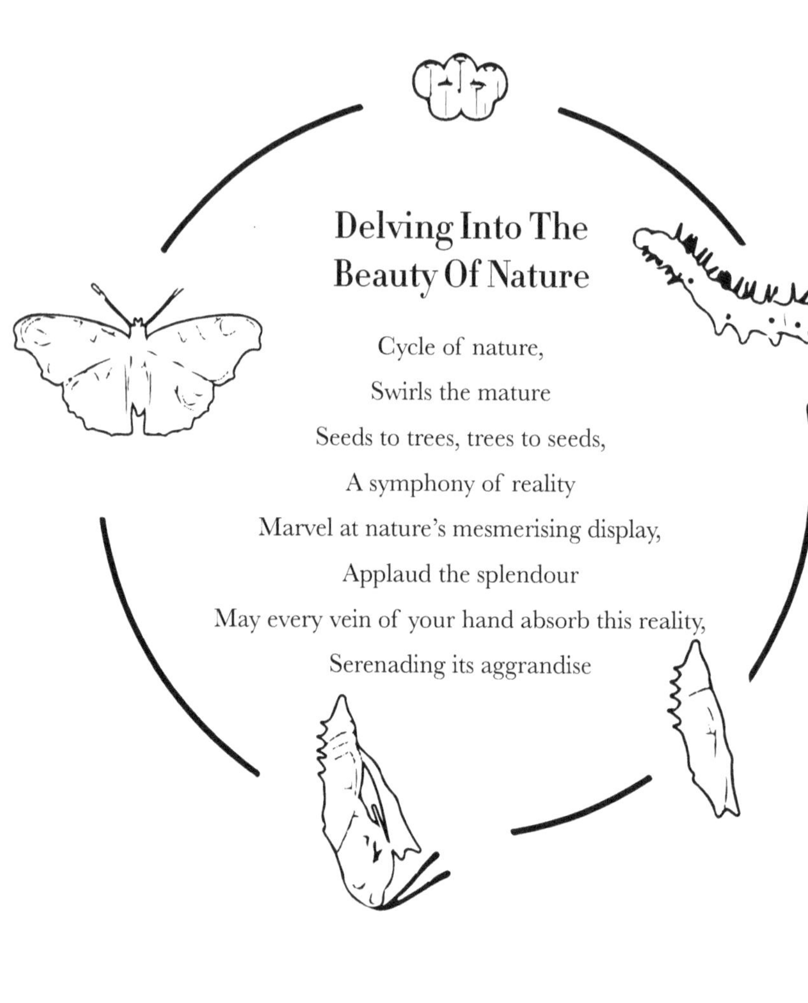

In the elegant dance of the natural world, there exists a timeless rhythm weaving through the fabric of existence with mesmerising grace and precision. This cyclic nature of nature, with its seasons of growth, decay, and rebirth, is a testament to the inherent wisdom and harmony that pervades the universe. Admiring it fosters a sense of humility and reverence for the resilience and adaptability inherent in the natural world.

Dear Me

You are adorable,

Stuffed with able

You are admiring,

Graced with vibrant shining

Let me love you,

For it is just for you

Let me nurture your body, a temple divine,

With care, patience, and sweet sunshine

As you treat yourself with love, you begin to realise that you are special—not because of what you do or what you achieve, but simply because of who you are. Treat yourself with the same love and care that you would offer to a cherished friend, and watch as your life blossoms with joy, fulfilment, and inner peace.

Days Of Dilemma

Some are the days;

I feel like strangers at away,

Distancing my embracing self

Some are the days;

I feel the strong bond at play,

Germinating my culminating self

Between this struggle of answering my queries,

Lies the routine to bliss and eerie

Carving way to ethereal road,

Lending you hand to row your boat

There's a delicate balance in the dance between solitude and companionship—a rhythm that ebbs and flows with the tides of our emotions and experiences. Sometimes, the solitude feels like a warm embrace but then there are times when the solitude feels less like a refuge and more like a void. However, it is not a sign of weakness but of courage and readiness to embrace new beginnings. It takes strength to acknowledge the times when you just need me time but also embracing our need for connection. Let us celebrate the duality of our nature—the joy of solitude and the comfort of companionship

The April

A gentle breeze whispers through,
Carrying scents of earth anew
For in its beauty, we find our way,
To hope, to joy, to a brighter day

APRIL

S M T W T F S

Blossoming Camouflaged Positivity

A storm of butterflies,

Transcends hard to utter

Words of positivity,

Bereft of guise,

Listen them with your heart full of compassion

Despite intricate court's thoughts,

Promise to sail in optimistic boat

With every sunrise, a new day is born,

Lending chance to grow, shine and adorn

Sustaining a positive demeanour necessitates the cultivation of an optimistic mindset, fortified by cognitive resilience and an unwavering commitment to adversarial transcendence. It entails the adept navigation of complexities with an equipoised disposition, characterised by fortitude, sagacity, and perspicacity.

Embrace The Life As It Comes

Every moment holds something new,

Try not to change as it dew

Let future be esoteric,

Mysterious enough to be majestic

Welcome the unknown waiting along,

In the tapestry of time for long

Embracing life with open arms, trusting in the wisdom of the universe and the natural order of things is acknowledging the inherent beauty in its unpredictability. Let us release the need to control outcomes and instead surrender to the flow of life, allowing it to lead us on a journey of self-discovery, growth, and fulfilment. For in the acceptance of life as it comes, we find freedom, peace, and the courage to live fully in the present moment.

A Pause

Everything happens for a cause,

Because it asks for a pause

You deserve the best,

Just hold the rest

It's difficult to wait,

But worse to regret late

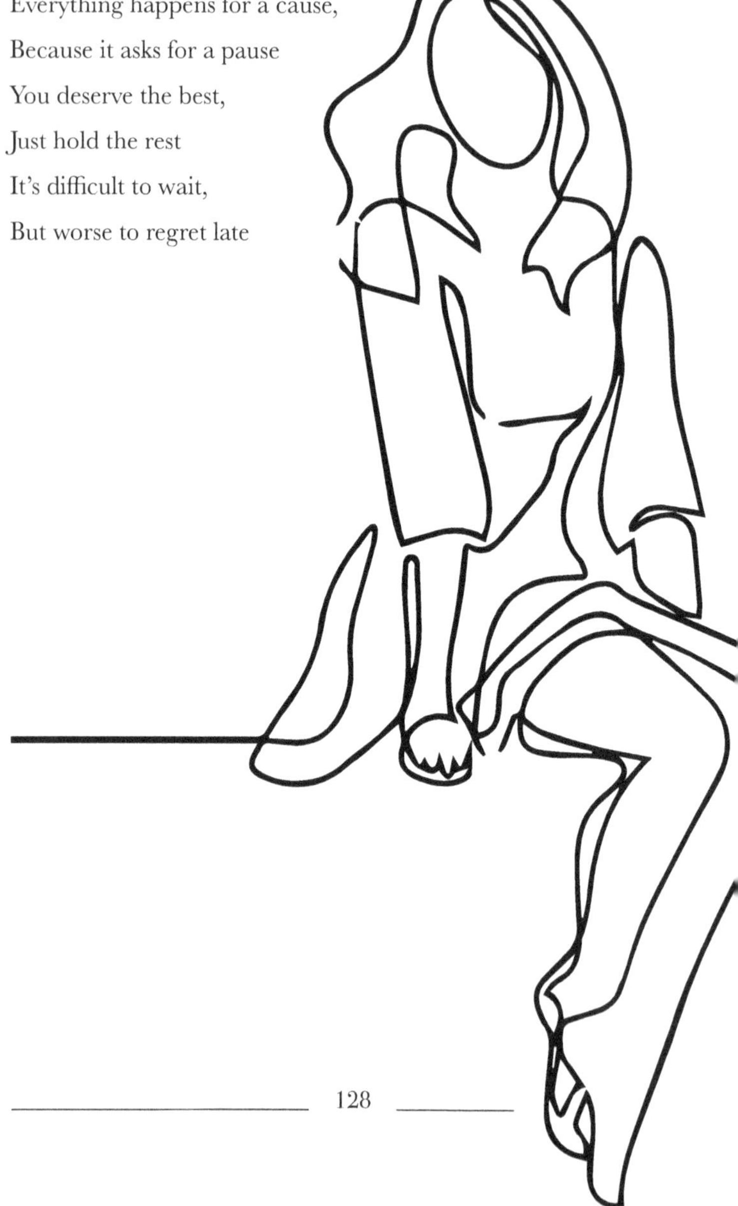

In the grand symphony of life, there's a reassuring melody that whispers through the chaos—an assurance that everything happens for a cause, and that each moment unfolds with purpose and precision. Waiting for the right moment is not a passive act but an act of courage and wisdom—an acknowledgment that some things are worth waiting for, worth nurturing, worth fighting for. Like a seed planted in fertile soil, waiting for the perfect conditions to sprout and grow, we too must cultivate patience and resilience as we wait for the right moment to bloom.It's about trusting the natural rhythm of life, the divine timing that orchestrates the unfolding of our dreams and aspirations.

The May

It is filled with care,
For it planted new lives
It has the melody filled air,
And, each dawn is a blissful flair

MAY

S	M	T	W	T	F	S

Waiting For The One

I am waiting

For the evergreen phrases,

That you somehow embrace

For the moments of calmness,

That assure your presence harness

True love will always run,

For you, my destined one

Waiting for new bonds to form can be a period of anticipation, but it's also a time of quiet reassurance. Amidst the gentle cadence of waiting, there's a soothing calmness that permeates the soul, a tranquil oasis where patience meets the promise of companionship. In the stillness of this waiting, there's a sense of trust in the universe's unfolding plan. It's a reminder that every connection, every bond, arrives in its own time.

From End To Start

Days held my heart,
Weeks sew a new art
Scars on my hand,
Healed with a time band
Just like the throbbing pain,
Left my flesh sane
A chapter I closed,
Carved deep furrows disclosed
A chapter new opened,
To tribute the hope proposed

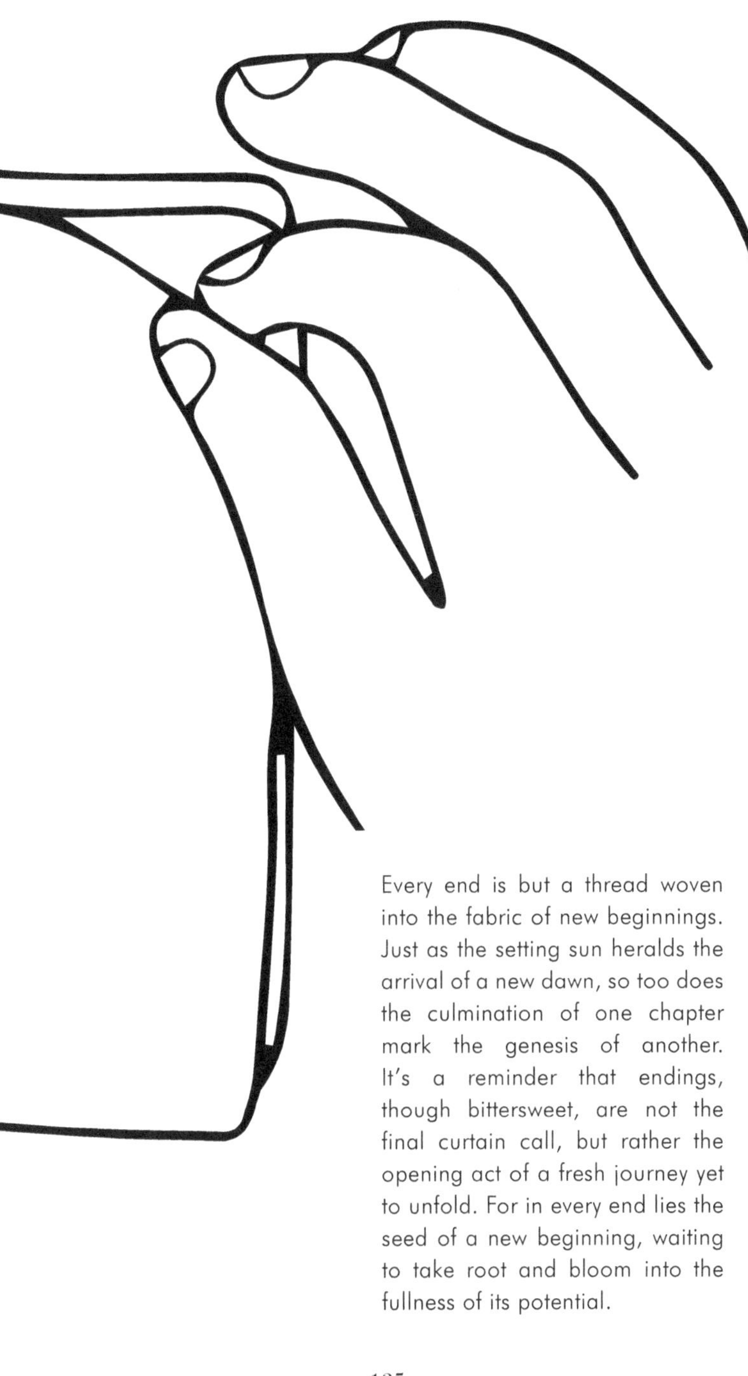

Every end is but a thread woven into the fabric of new beginnings. Just as the setting sun heralds the arrival of a new dawn, so too does the culmination of one chapter mark the genesis of another. It's a reminder that endings, though bittersweet, are not the final curtain call, but rather the opening act of a fresh journey yet to unfold. For in every end lies the seed of a new beginning, waiting to take root and bloom into the fullness of its potential.

I Now Cherish

The soothing voice that makes you whole,
Calms down every corner of my soul
Making me sing all my secrets fraught,
Carving your forever thought

The comfort in your eyes,
Carries to the mystery cries
And, sparkles the little me,
Who wanders like an immature bee

The generous heart that always shine,
Mirrors the purity of divine
Seeing yours make me skip my beat fast,
As if this is our day last

The hands that embrace mine
Persuades your eternal touch shine
It holds me tightly,
And, adores me softly

Today is about the breath we share,
Tomorrow will be about the soul we will share

I fall and rise everyday above,
For your immortal love
Clearing all the held dues,
And the cycle continues

It was **spring** then,
When my world started
But it will be **autumn** far,
When my world will end

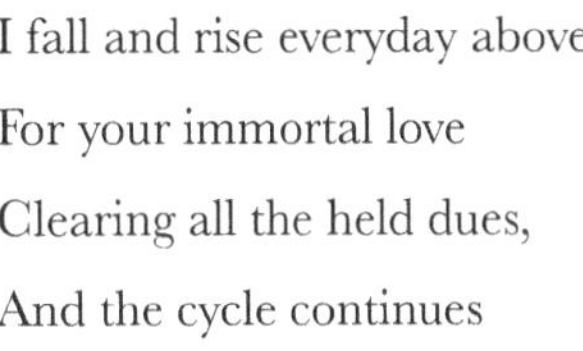

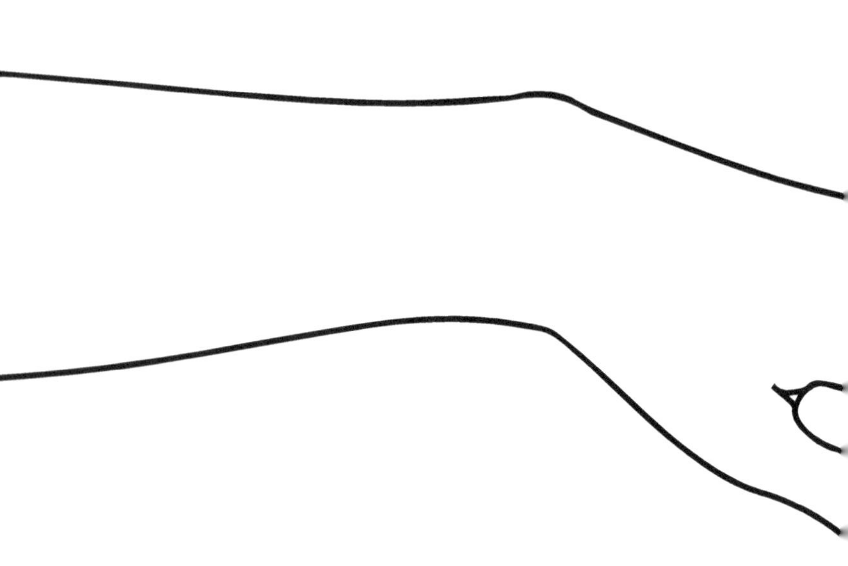

Relationship is about cherishing not just the grand gestures, but also the everyday gestures. Every quirk, every idiosyncrasy becomes a thread in the tapestry of our affection, weaving a bond that transcends the ordinary. From the way they absentmindedly twirl their hair to the sound of their laughter echoing through the air, lies beauty in the simplest of gestures for it weaves a lovely mansion.

Cherishing small gestures is what ways to bliss. It is not always about the shiny things that can make you content but sometimes a handmade card also works.

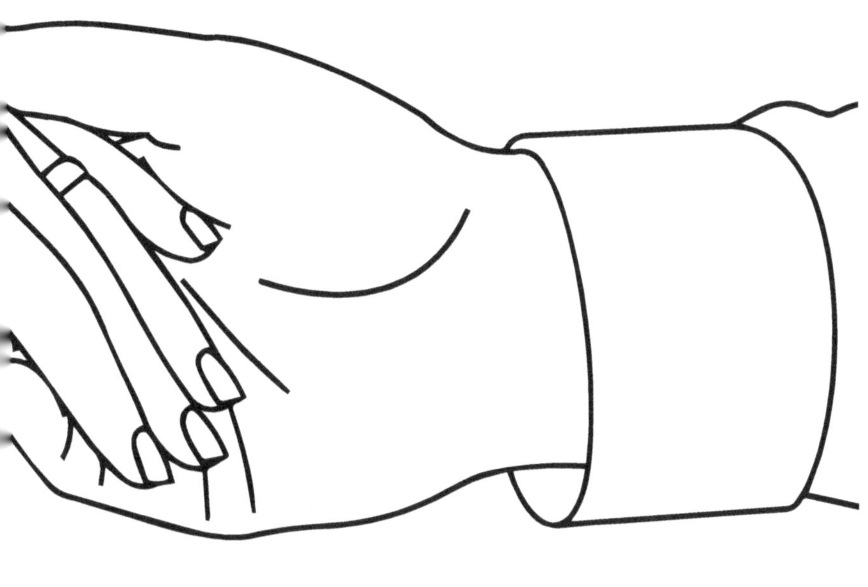

And, the cycle continues, from end to start, from falling in love to staring at the moon, missing them and coming out stronger again. From letting go of what no longer serves us in **Autumn** to actually preparing the soil for new beginnings to take roots by dealing with the shadows, cloaked in the darkness of solitude and reflection that **Winter** brings along and by finally revelling in the warmth of **Summer** and basking in the glow of shared experiences to again cater strength to start afresh in **Spring**.